Wrestling with God

Messages for Lent & Easter
on the Life of Jacob

Wrestling
with
God

VERNON R. SCHREIBER

AUGSBURG Publishing House • Minneapolis

WRESTLING WITH GOD

Contents

Preface

Have you wondered where you are headed? Do you feel you are getting nowhere? Do you wish you knew what you could do about it? It may surprise you to know that one of the most famous figures in religious history wrestled with God over the same kinds of questions. His name was Jacob, the Jacob you dimly remember from your Sunday school days but have not thought about since. He has become a man who seems to have little to do with your life today.

On the basis of my own study and the response of parish members to a series of sermons on the crises in his life, I have become convinced that Jacob deserves far more attention than he gets from any of us. His is one of those fascinating case histories which make up so large a part of the Holy Scriptures. He found out about life the hard way. He had trouble making it in business and in marriage. He had trouble praying. He wrestled with God in so many areas of life, just as we do. But he never gave up until at last he found himself—or maybe it is better to say, until he was found by God.

So I invite you to look at his life as a case history which will help you understand your own behavior and feelings. Furthermore, through Jacob we have not only an opportunity to understand ourselves better, but to understand more fully the way God deals with us—an ingredient which is always present in case histories from the Scriptures.

I also believe that Jacob fits into Lenten reflections because his actions, like those of Peter, Mary Magdalene, Judas, Pilate, and a host of others, illuminate how we react to the presence of the God of love. More importantly, he shows us how the God who is love reacts to us and our ways, a reaction finally climaxing in the giving of his Son, Jesus.

I have seen people respond to Jacob as a powerful example of what it means to fall and then be lifted up again, to doubt and find faith restored, and to turn away from God and then return again with a far deeper commitment. Jacob compels us to see together how we all struggle with God until we find that we can have no peace apart from a surrender to his love. I invite you to discover through these Lenten messages how we can all become new people through our wrestling with God.

¹⁸ So he went in to his father, and said, "My father"; and he said, "Here I am; who are you, my son?" ¹⁹ Jacob said to his father, "I am Esau your firstborn. I have done as you told me; now sit up and eat of my game, that you may bless me." ²⁰ But Isaac said to his son, "How is it that you have found it so quickly, my son?" He answered, "Because the Lord your God granted me success." ²¹ Then Isaac said to Jacob, "Come near, that I may feel you, my son, to know whether you are really my son Esau or not." ²² So Jacob went near to Isaac his father, who felt him and said, "The voice is Jacob's voice, but the hands are the hands of Esau." ²³ And he did not recognize him, because his hands were hairy like his brother Esau's hands; so he blessed him. ²⁴ He said, "Are you really my son Esau?" He answered, "I am." ²⁵ Then he said, "Bring it to me, that I may eat of my son's game and bless you." So he brought it to him, and he ate; and he brought him wine, and he drank. ²⁶ Then his father Isaac said to him, "Come near and kiss me, my son." ²⁷ So he came near and kissed him; and he smelled the smell of his garments, and blessed him, and said,

"See, the smell of my son is as the smell of a field which the Lord has blessed! ²⁸ May God give you of the dew of heaven, and of the fatness of the earth, and plenty of grain and wine. ²⁹ Let peoples serve you, and nations bow down to you. Be lord over your brothers, and may your mother's sons bow down to you. Cursed be every one who curses you, and blessed be every one who blesses you!"

Genesis 27:18-29
Parallel readings: Ps. 119:33-40; Matt. 26:47-56

1

Leave a Little to God

The problem of forcing the will of God instead of becoming a part of it

A man walked into my office. He was desperate. He had to talk to someone. The business recession had caught up with him. His customers, small business people themselves, depended on him for credit. He depended on them to pay him back somehow so that he could pay his own creditors. It was the old story. They didn't and he didn't. Now everything was coming down on him at once.

"What are your feelings?" I asked him.

"I'm angry," he said. Then his voice rose to a higher level of intensity. "I'm angry as hell. I'm angry with God. I've always believed in him. From the very first day I started my business I prayed that he would bless it. After all, the only reason I am in this is to provide my family with happiness and a little security. What's so wrong with that? Why couldn't he answer my prayers?"

"What are you going to do?" I asked.

"I'm not sure. I tell you, there are moments when I am ready to try anything to keep this thing afloat. It just isn't fair the way things are turning out!"

Forcing the Will of God

As I listened to my friend, I thought of another man who had much the same problem. His name was Jacob. Jacob is revered and honored as one of the patriarchs of the Old Testament; but for all his fame, he had a great deal of trouble handling this basic question of life: "Am I forcing the will of God or becoming a part of it?"

This is a real problem for all of us. In fact, Jacob wrestled with God over many of the problems of life which we experience. This is why we are going to take a close look at his life during this season of Lent. He is a man who can help us understand ourselves much more clearly, and there is no better place to begin on this Ash Wednesday than with the whole matter of truly fitting ourselves into the will and purposes of God. For while we, as religious people, talk a great deal about the will of God, how much do we really understand the obedience of Christ which led to his passion and death? How much are we able to accept into our lives the Father's will that there must be a crucifixion before there can be a resurrection?

Like that businessman, Jacob was wrestling with God over the fact that certain blessings which ought to have been coming his way were too slow in arriving. He was certain that he should be on top. He believed that it was clearly God's will that he should be first and Esau, his twin brother, second. There was no arguing that Esau had come out of their mother's womb first, but had not the Lord said to Rebekah, "The elder shall serve the younger" (Gen. 25:23)? Furthermore, it probably seemed quite obvious to Jacob, the quiet and intellectual type, that he would be a better leader of the clan than Esau—who was always taking off on a hunting trip. The thought kept pounding away in Jacob's brain, "*I* am number one!"

So the day arrived when Isaac—now blind, and his other senses failing as well—wished to give his final and best blessing to Esau. He told Esau to go out, shoot some game, and bring it to him that he might eat it and then bless him before he died. It was at this point that Rebekah went into action. As soon as Esau was outside the camp she told Jacob to bring a meal to his blind father and get the blessing for himself. At first

Jacob was afraid, but Rebekah insisted. If the saying had been popular at the time, she probably would have told him, "God helps those who help themselves." She gave Jacob Esau's clothes, disguised him, put a bowl of savory food in his hands, and pointed him towards Isaac's tent. Once he was inside Jacob joined wholeheartedly in this attempt to bring to quick fulfillment the promises of God. When Isaac, not a little suspicious, asked how Esau could have gotten back so quickly with the game, Jacob replied with a great show of piety, "Because the Lord your God granted me success" (Gen. 27:20). The faker!

A Mirror of Our Own Impatience

But wait. It is precisely at this point that we must use the Bible as a mirror to show us our own selves. There is an old Jewish saying, "Leave a little to God!"; but we do not want to listen to this advice any more than Jacob did. How often haven't we felt that we must force a solution which will guarantee God's blessings? How often haven't we been tempted to use the argument, "If we don't take matters into our own hands, how will we who are God's people ever get what he has promised us?" We focus on the problem instead of on God. While it may be nice to talk about faith and all that, we still want to make sure that things turn out the way we planned. We become "Jacobs" who feel that it is our calling to outmaneuver the "Esaus" blocking our way to a successful life.

Coming Up with Nothing

"Jacobs" do not really fare too well. As Jesus warned Peter, "All who take the sword will perish by the sword" (Matt. 26:52). The first Jacob discovered that. He had bargained Esau out of the rights of the firstborn. Then he had tricked Isaac into giving him the best blessing. It must have appeared to him that his destiny was secure. Now God's promises were sure to come to pass. That's what *he* thought! There was one little problem he had not counted on. Esau announced that there would soon be not one but two funerals in the family. He swore aloud, "The days of mourning for my father are approaching; then I will kill my brother Jacob" (Gen. 27:41). In their terror Jacob and Rebekah could think of only one thing to do. Jacob would have to flee the country to save his skin.

So it goes. If we think that it is up to us to write our own script on how life shall unfold for us, there are always others who have developed their own scenarios which smash ours to pieces. It is no accident that one of the most familiar

sayings is, "Out of the frying pan into the fire."
Our efforts to grab a blessing turn on us. The
girl who schemes to steal a boy from her best
friend discovers that he is the type who always
needs someone new to be making a play for him.
The boss whom a man has carefully cultivated
leaves, and the new manager makes it clear he
wants to build a team with no old loyalties. Or
the market for which a man was willing to sell his
soul dries up. There is no rest for those who grasp
after the blessings they feel should rightfully be
coming their way.

Time after time in the Lenten history of our
Lord's suffering we see people who wanted to
force a solution to the problems they saw. The
high priest explained that he was really doing
the right thing and serving the best interests of
God's people by getting rid of Jesus. It must
have appeared to him that everything was
going to work out splendidly after he made his
deal with Judas. Perhaps he even offered up a
lovely prayer of thanksgiving. Peace at last! Certain scholars have conjectured that the betrayal
of Jesus was itself an effort by Judas to force
God's hand and thus quickly bring about the
promised coming of the Son of man in all his
glory. We all remember how Peter whipped out
his sword, as God's answer to the vicious crowd
pressing in on Jesus. He began to use it, too. Yes,

the Bible is filled with case histories of people who became so intent on solving God's problems that they ended up disregarding God himself. It happens all the time. It happens to us.

A Better Man and a Better Way

Jesus knew the better way. He saw the subtle but profoundly important difference between seeking to force the will of God and becoming a part of it. This is why his behavior at the time of his arrest in the Garden of Gethsemane was so radically different. He held on to the promises of God in a situation which seemed to deny the trustworthiness of every promise ever made to him. Whatever the Father had said in the past about Jesus being his beloved Son, where was that Father now? Was not his absence a sign that the Son should take it upon himself to show his own power and glory? As Jesus' enemies—their torches held high—came crashing into that garden, it is easy to imagine him thinking that he should call for 12 legions of angels to come to his side against this rotten crew.

At least that is what the Tempter would have suggested, and the fact that Jesus mentions those angels at the very moment he tells Peter to put away his sword suggests that Jesus was very much aware of the help they could have given.

Furthermore, Jesus could have argued that he was not really looking for his own glory and safety but was only interested in promoting the long-range plans of God! As the firstborn of God (Col. 1:15) why not claim at that very moment the world and its kingdoms as his proper inheritance? He could have done that. But he did not do it. His "food" was to be a part of the Father's will (John 4:34), nothing more and nothing less. If it was the will of the Father that he be a Messiah who would endure rejection, abandonment, and (according to Jewish belief) an unclean death upon a cross, so be it. It was his choice to be a part of the Father's will to provide a Savior for all people.

Conformed to the Will of the Father

The consequence of this free choice by Jesus is that now you and I can be free at last to trust God in all circumstances. We do not need to reach certain goals in order to prove to ourselves that his blessing rests upon us. We know that he has already qualified us to be named his children. We can give "thanks to the Father, who has qualified us to share in the inheritance of the saints in light" (Col. 1:12). We know to whom we belong. Belonging to him, we know that already we have everything. Instead of describing the will of God in terms of what we think ought to be happening, we talk about what sort of persons we want to be.

When we repent of our forcing God's will and desire instead to become a part of it—even if it leads to a cross—a whole new world opens to us. I spoke earlier about meeting with a distraught businessman. As we talked, the subject moved around to both Jesus and Jacob. In that conversation the Bible became once again the living Word of God. My friend saw his impatience. He also saw how he could accept his life that day as a fresh gift from God, with Jesus as the center of God's gifts. When he had accepted his life in this way, he turned it back to God for his safekeeping. This may sound like a rather fundamental and even commonplace decision, but it is the biggest step any of us can take. It is a decision that enables us at last to admit to God that while we are no good at all in deciding what events should take place in the future, such matters could not be in better hands than those of him who died for us. It is enough to be his instrument. It is in such a decision that both the cross and the resurrection become possible.

¹⁰ Jacob left Beersheba, and went toward Haran. ¹¹ And he came to a certain place, and stayed there that night, because the sun had set. Taking one of the stones of the place, he put it under his head and lay down in that place to sleep.

¹² And he dreamed that there was a ladder set up on the earth, and the top of it reached to heaven; and behold, the angels of God were ascending and descending on it! ¹³ And behold, the Lord stood above it and said, "I am the Lord, the God of Abraham your father and the God of Isaac; the land on which you lie I will give to you and to your descendants; ¹⁴ and your descendants shall be like the dust of the earth, and you shall spread abroad to the west and to the east and to the north and to the south; and by you and your descendants shall all the families of the earth bless themselves. ¹⁵ Behold, I am with you and will keep you wherever you go, and will bring you back to this land; for I will not leave you until I have done that of which I have spoken to you."

¹⁶ Then Jacob awoke from his sleep and said, "Surely the Lord is in this place; and I did not know it." ¹⁷ And he was afraid, and said, "How awesome is this place! This is none other than the house of God, and this is the gate of heaven."

Genesis 28:10-17
Parallel readings: Psalm 139; John 1:43-51

2

Who Let Down
the Ladder?

*The problem of how
communion with God begins*

Lent is a time when we talk a great deal about getting close to God. We stress the devotional life. We encourage self-discipline. In the process we can also foster some mistaken ideas about what makes communion with God possible. We think we are the ones who get it going. Who is close to God? Who does God talk to? Why, this is the experience of the saintly, of course! If there is going to be a ladder between us and God, then we must be the spiritual carpenters.

This outlook makes it difficult for us to truly hear and learn from a most familiar Bible story, often referred to as "Jacob's Ladder." According to our standards, that ladder must have been there because Jacob was such a great man. But Jacob was *not* a great man. He wrecked everything he touched. He tricked his brother out of the rights of the firstborn. He deceived his father and secured for himself the blessing due his brother. He reduced his entire family to a junk heap of broken relationships. Since most of us would have difficulty in even talking to such a scoundrel, the thought that Jacob should be given a splendid vision of God ought also to strike us as totally unreasonable and unfair.

Nor is there any evidence that Jacob himself expected any manifestation of a heavenly ladder. Some people have speculated that in this dream Jacob was simply projecting the expectations of his own ambitious ego. Such speculation does not fit with the mood that must have engulfed Jacob. He was alone and afraid. He had been forced to flee from his home for fear of his life. But his fears went even deeper than the fear of Esau's vengeance or of the darkness of the wilderness. He was haunted by the knowledge that he had done wrong. He had possessed enough inner honesty to admit this when he said to his mother, "If my father happens to touch me, he will see I am cheating him . . ." (Gen. 27:12 JB). Knowing him to be filled with this awareness of his guilt, there is no reason to imagine that he even said a little "Now I lay me down to sleep" before he rested his head against a boulder and slept. He was a man in total spiritual isolation.

God Lets Down the Ladder

There is only one explanation for what happened next. We do not build a ladder to God. It is God who lets down the ladder to us. Yes, it was a dream, but one in which God provided the content—enabling Jacob to find meaning beyond what his ordinary senses could have told him. The content of that dream shows us that the gospel of Genesis is the same as the gospel of John. God is the God of grace. He takes the initiative. He reaches down to the sinner. He renews his promise to a rascal as unworthy as Jacob.

Beyond the Ladder Is the Promise

It is difficult to keep our attention focused on the promise that God was making as Jacob dreamed of the ladder from heaven. We tend to get hung up on the ladder. After all, from early childhood we have been taught to be impressed by "spectaculars." The Sunday school image of Jacob's ladder which sticks in our mind is not unlike one of those splendid staircases in an old Hollywood musical, with gorgeous angels floating gracefully up and down until—behold!—the star is spotlighted at the very top of it. For most of us this picture blots out the real significance of that special moment. We are so dazzled by the picture that we lose sight of the fact that he who is perfectly holy has chosen to speak a word of promise to a human being who is not even a good person. Jacob has shown neither elementary honesty nor any real trust in God. He is exactly like you and me. But God makes his promise anyway. Part of this promise has already been spoken to Abraham and Isaac. Now God lets it be known that he will still keep it through a wretch like Jacob, and makes it more personal than ever. Not only will Jacob's descendants inherit the ground on which he slept, but God will be with Jacob in whatever happens and will never forsake him.

God Comes Down to Us

Do we see what this says about God? It means that we can believe that he will speak and keep his word of promise to us, not because we deserve it, but because his way is the way of forgiveness and restoration. We may be undeserving and unlovable, but we are so important to him that he lets down the ladder and comes to us. That is why the Bible has been given to us. It tells us that God speaks in the same way and for the same reason today as he spoke to people in days of old. We simply do not understand the Bible at all if we do not understand this. It is the story of God invading the very center of our existence because he wants to find us, speak to us, and bring us back to himself; and the message of the Christian gospel is that the most profound disclosure of his heart took place through his Son, Jesus Christ. The passion history tells us about the climax of that invasion. It shows us God in Christ speaking his word of promise to men and women who, like Jacob, are trying to escape from their past.

Jesus himself once made an explicit comparison between his presence on earth and the story of Jacob's ladder. He said to a man he was recruiting for discipleship, "Nathaniel, you have been impressed mightily because you see that I can look into your heart. But that is nothing compared to what you will see. You will see heaven opened, and the angels of God ascending and descending upon the Son of man" (cf. John 1:43-51). Jesus was alluding to the very event which had occurred in Jacob's life, but note the change in position which had taken place! God is no longer at the top of the ladder. He is at the bottom. He is here with us. He is clothed in the rough cloth of our own humanity. He is no longer restricted to an awesome and otherworldly revelation of his glory. He is one of us. He is Jesus, who did not count equality with God a thing to be grasped, but emptied himself and took upon himself the form of a servant.

Do we keep wishing for some special vision which will show us God? Are we like Philip, who rather pathetically said, "Show us the Father and we shall be satisfied" (John 14:8)? To him and to all of us this is the nature of Jesus' reply: "You say, 'Show us the Father'? Have you not seen me become the companion of the rejected of this world? Have I been with you all this time for nothing? How can you ask such a question? He who has seen me has seen the Father" (cf. John 14:8-9). Jesus is God at the bottom of the ladder, right here with us. Jesus is God's word of promise in the flesh: "The Father who lives in me carries out his work through me" (cf. John 14:10). Through Jesus God speaks, pardons, bears our guilt, and cleanses us. The Father has made Jesus the gate of heaven for each of us.

The Gate Is Open

Shaken to the roots by his experience, Jacob was filled with awe, and he said, "Truly the Lord was in this place and I never knew it! This is the gate of heaven!" (cf. Gen. 28:16-17). Jacob may have thought mistakenly that this was the only gate to heaven, but at least he knew what had happened. A divine invasion had taken place.

This experience should lead us to look at the potential of our own spiritual experience with great expectations. We need not limit ourselves to talking about how someday people may go to heaven. We can talk about how the transcendent God made himself known in a moment when Jacob would have thought God to be very far away. We can make this experience the foundation of our own hope and expectation. God in his mercy lets down the ladder. God in his love opens the gate which leads to himself.

God still opens the gate. A young couple named Carl and Loretta can tell how this happened one day for Carl. Carl was a young husband whose goal in life was providing every earthly comfort for his beautiful wife. It took all of his time, but no one could deny that he was reaching his goal. He was much like Jacob, self-serving and overly ambitious perhaps, but very good at getting what he was after. Loretta's lot in life was limited to accepting the prizes he brought home to her.

Then they became involved in a movement called "Marriage Encounter." They began to learn how to share their feelings. One day they were going to share their responses to the question, "How do I feel about God?" In telling his story Carl emphasized that he had been an expert in thinking up reasons which showed how foolish it was to believe in God. But this question did not ask him what he thought or invite him to argue about the thoughts of others. It challenged him to express his *feelings* about God. This time, instead of exercising his intellect, he discovered God opening up his heart and leading him to speak. He found himself expressing words of love for the Father and the Son. Deep feelings never before expressed poured out in a torrent of words. Their living room became a gate of heaven. Carl is now a man who knows that God is with him. Loretta knows it, too.

Without a doubt there are many ways by which God makes wide the gate to himself and speaks a word of promise which is never forgotten. But in the end all those ways converge in the picture which the season of Lent puts before us in Jesus Christ, crucified and risen again. Through him who came to rescue us, all things become new. They become gates of heaven. Through him bread and wine become the means of receiving him for our souls' benefit. Through him the Bible becomes holy ground on which we meet a forgiving God. Through him Lent becomes more than a season of TV reruns for people who do not want to go beyond being spectators. It becomes a rallying point for people who discover new gates opening to God. Through him our life becomes what the rocky hillside was for Jacob—the opportunity for a sinner to hear God speak anew his word of pardon and promise.

Do we build the ladder to God or does he come down to us? He comes to us, again and again. The darkness surrounding a frightened and forlorn Jacob was filled with the presence of God. The darkness of our own world of sin has been pierced once and for all by Jesus Christ. By faith in him who came down to earth to die upon a cross, communion with God can become real and alive. To whom does the Lord speak? To the saintly and the devout? Yes, of course. But he also speaks to you and to me. In Jesus, the Lord of Love, he is speaking right now.

²⁰ So Jacob served seven years for Rachel, and they seemed to him but a few days because of the love he had for her. . . .

¹ When Rachel saw that she bore Jacob no children, she envied her sister; and she said to Jacob, "Give me children, or I shall die!" ² Jacob's anger was kindled against Rachel, and he said, "Am I in the place of God, who has withheld from you the fruit of the womb?"

Genesis 29:20; 30:1-2
Parallel readings: Psalm 127; John 19:23-27

3

A Stranger
in My Tent

**The problem of establishing
Christian expectations for my marriage**

One man, when asked, "How is your wife?" likes to respond, "Compared to what?" He is saying that if his answer is to have any meaning, it must be specific. There must be a standard of comparison. If we are asked, "How is your marriage?" it does not hurt to respond with the same question: "Compared to what?" Compared to the marriage of an apparently radiant and successful couple we see at certain parties? Compared to a perfect marriage? Compared to the marriage we thought we would have? Here is a fundamental question with which we must wrestle. What kind of marriage are we asking from God? Are we asking for a perfect marriage or a Christian marriage?

A Stranger in My Tent

The love story of Jacob and Rachel can help us a great deal in understanding what we ought to be looking for in marriage and family life. In this story we find two people whose marriage was not working out at all as they had hoped. They had gone through so much to become husband and wife that you would expect a "happily ever after" ending to have followed quite naturally. It definitely did not.

To review the story of Jacob, when he arrived at the home of his uncle, Laban, it looked like great blessings were about to come his way. Soon, however, it became apparent that the promises of God did not include a smooth road to matrimony. The fact is, Jacob awoke to find himself married to a stranger, and this happened not once, but twice.

The first disappointment followed a wild and joyous wedding ceremony. Jacob had fallen so deeply in love with Rachel that he had promised to work for Laban seven years if only she could be his bride. Gladness filled his heart as he stood next to his heavily veiled bride. Spirits ran high. Then came the morning after. As Jacob focused his eyes in the morning light, he discovered a stranger in his tent! The girl next to him was not the lovely Rachel, but her sister, lackluster

Leah. Only after Jacob agreed to work an additional seven years did he receive Rachel as well.

But we said that Jacob discovered a stranger in his tent a second time. This happened on the occasion of his discovering what all married people discover. It happened at or before the bitter exchange between Jacob and Rachel which the Scriptures have recorded for us. It happened as Jacob found himself saying, "I thought I knew Rachel, but I didn't know she was going to be like this!" Rachel had her own reasons for thinking the same. How could a man who had been willing to work for a total of 14 years in order to have her as his wife at the same time be so indifferent to her misery and angrily shout at her, "Am I in the place of God, who has withheld from you the fruit of the womb?" (Gen. 30:2). They were making the discovery common to young married people. It is not finding love but staying in love that is the hard part.

Unfulfilled Expectations

The things that were splitting Jacob and Rachel apart were the problems which are common to all of us in our own tents. First of all, they were torn apart by an unfulfilled expectation. This is such a basic fault. Much of the sin which mars our relationship with others begins right here. We expect too much. We want everything to work perfectly. We do not want to face the fact that marriage is not an arm-in-arm stroll into an unending sunset where there is no disillusionment, no misunderstanding, no thinning hair, no bulge in the midriff, no financial disappointments—especially compared to the people next door. We want to possess a type of solid-state love not unlike that of a modern TV or radio set. Flip a switch and love goes on instantly, without any need for warming up. Maybe that is a characteristic of what we dream to be the "perfect" marriage, but it is not a part of a Christian marriage. In a Christian marriage two people know that love cannot be frozen and kept in some kind of container outside the daily exchanges of life. Love needs regular exchanges between two people, exchanges which do not always reveal the best in us, but are nevertheless the only soil in which love can grow.

Shortcuts to Happiness

Some people also see the ideal marriage as one in which they will be able to find easy shortcuts to the happiness they desire. It is significant that the same chapter which tells us of the growing gap between Jacob and Rachel tells us of Rachel's pathetic search for an instant remedy.

One day she saw Leah's son, Reuben, coming in from the fields carrying a handful of mandrakes. Mandrakes were a rare kind of plant which the people of that time believed could be made into a love potion. In desperation Rachel offered Leah a little more time with Jacob in exchange for these mandrakes. She hoped that *they* might work where *she* had been failing. Today most people do not buy something labeled, "Love Potion" (unless you count deodorants, perfume, after-shave lotion, and toothpaste), but we do see the world filled with offers of one technique after the other, each guaranteeing that *this* will be the approach which will bring instant love and everlasting happiness. Millions of magazines and books are bought in the hope that a shortcut will be found which does not really require a change within ourselves.

Settling for Something Less than Love

When some people cannot find the perfect marriage they are looking for, they try to settle for something less. They decide that it may be enough if they can simply be good parents—as if you can be good parents when you are not lovers! There is a poster which every man ought to own: "The best thing a father can do for his children is to love their mother." It is true, as commentaries like to point out, that through the bitter competition between Rachel and Leah God provided Jacob with 12 stalwart sons, the very foundation of the future nation of Israel. But so much was lacking because of the breakdown of love. The fact that Jacob hated Leah had disastrous consequences for everyone (Gen. 29:31). For the day would come when the sons of Leah would have so little regard for the father who despised their mother that they would be willing to murder Joseph, the first and long-awaited son of Rachel and Jacob (Gen. 37:18-20). It can be better for children not to see their parents together at all than to see them in a bond of hate. Nor is hate the only opposite of love. Apathy and indifference can serve just as well as destructive forces within our tent.

Our Fundamental Testing Ground

A Christian marriage, however, does not calmly settle for half a loaf any more than it demands perfection. It recognizes that this fundamental experience called marriage is often the basic testing ground for our faithfulness to God. We might wish for a more dramatic field on which to prove our worth. We might indulge in the fantasy of being in the company of the disciples when Jesus was arrested—standing our ground while all others fled. But that is escapism. Scripture reminds us that if we cannot love the people we see, we cannot love God whom we do not see (1 John 4:20).

The Power to Love

To prevail in those tests which our day-to-day relationships with others give us, we need no less a capacity for love than Jesus had. For Jesus was never surprised at the human blend of goodness and evil, commitment and faithlessness, sacrifice and selfishness, promises and betrayal. Those who were closest to him would wound him the most deeply. He knew that. "I tell you, Peter, the cock will not crow this day, until you three times deny that you know me" (Luke 22:34). Yet he did not pull away from them. He loved them to the end. He possessed a love which had staying power, able to restore and heal after very real and deep wounds had been inflicted against him. This is the love we need.

Where shall we find the power to love in such a manner? Christians respond that there is no better way to tap into such power than through the experience of Christ in one's own life. This is where the Lenten story, which in itself seems to say so little about family and marital relations, actually says everything. It is the story of people who were filled with selfishness, fear, ambition, and lovelessness, and who completely failed each other as well as the God they professed to love. They were destroyed by the very attitudes which also destroy those relationships we call friendship or marriage.

Nevertheless, in the midst of such total and typical human failure, Jesus became the starting point for new relationships. He not only went into death as a victim of the very attitudes we must confess to God as our sins; but even as he was dying, he began to reach back from the cross to create new and better relationships. He said to Mary and the disciple whom he loved, " 'Woman, behold, your son!' Then he said to the disciple, 'Behold, your mother!' And from that hour the disciple took her to his own home" (John 19:26-27). When Jesus arose from the dead, he restored Peter and commissioned him to bring the whole flock together to be fed (John 21:15-19). He said to the others who had fled from their testing ground, "Peace. I forgive you. In my name go forth and proclaim new beginnings for everyone" (cf. John 20:19-23). To this day the living Christ gathers people around his table to share in his supper and to show the world that in him there is the power to restore the relationship of love.

Putting It Back Together through Christ

Is there a stranger in your tent? Sometimes there is in mine, and often I myself am that stranger. I try to wear a disguise. I fear being discovered, although that is inevitable. I become bitter or angry because my expectations have not been met. It is at times like these that the behavior in my tent has resembled the behavior of strangers, not lovers.

But by the power of Christ the story about life in the tent of any one of us does not need to stop with such a confession. The power of Jesus' love, discovered in the story of Lent and Easter, can also be present. It leads us to place ourselves again in the Upper Room where Jesus gave his final instructions to his followers: "A new commandment I give to you, that you love one another; even as I have loved you, that you also love one another" (John 13:34). He was speaking of much more than romantic feelings or duty-bound relationships. He was speaking of the love which gives us something better than a perfect marriage. It gives us a Christian marriage, ready to forgive, ready to bear a cross, and ready to pay a price without counting the cost. When this love takes hold, then Jesus has entered our tent; and through him new beginnings are made so that we live as strangers no more.

¹³ When Laban heard the tidings of Jacob his sister's son, he ran to meet him, and embraced him and kissed him, and brought him to his house. Jacob told Laban all these things, ¹⁴ and Laban said to him, "Surely you are my bone and my flesh!" And he stayed with him a month.

¹⁵ Then Laban said to Jacob, "Because you are my kinsman, should you therefore serve me for nothing? Tell me, what shall your wages be?" ¹⁶ Now Laban had two daughters; the name of the older was Leah, and the name of the younger was Rachel. ¹⁷ Leah's eyes were weak, but Rachel was beautiful and lovely. ¹⁸ Jacob loved Rachel; and he said, "I will serve you seven years for your younger daughter Rachel." ¹⁹ Laban said, "It is better that I give her to you than that I should give her to any other man; stay with me." ²⁰ So Jacob served seven years for Rachel, and they seemed to him but a few days because of the love he had for her.

²¹ Then Jacob said to Laban, "Give me my wife that I may go in to her, for my time is completed." ²² So Laban gathered together all the men of the place, and made a feast. ²³ But in the evening he took his daughter Leah and brought her to Jacob; and he went in to her. ²⁴ (Laban gave his maid Zilpah to his daughter Leah to be her maid.) ²⁵ And in the morning, behold, it was Leah; and Jacob said to Laban, "What is this you have done to me? Did I not serve with you for Rachel? Why then have you deceived me?" ²⁶ Laban said, "It is not so done in our country, to give the younger before the first-born. ²⁷ Complete the week of this one, and we will give you the other also in return for serving me another seven years." ²⁸ Jacob did so, and completed her week; then Laban gave him his daughter Rachel to wife. ²⁹ (Laban gave his maid Bilhah to his daughter Rachel to be her maid.) ³⁰ So Jacob went in to Rachel also, and he loved Rachel more than Leah, and served Laban for another seven years.

Genesis 29:13-30
Parallel readings: Psalm 72; Luke 19:1-10

4

What Is Profit and What Is Loss?

The problem of confronting a materialistic value system

In a portion of his hard-hitting song from the late sixties Ray Stevens says to "Mr. Businessman":

Did you see your children growing up today?
And did you hear the music of their laughter as they set about to play?
Do you qualify to be alive,
Or is the limit of your senses so as only to survive?
Spending counterfeit incentive, wasting precious time and health.
Placing value on the worthless, disregarding priceless wealth,
You can wheel and deal the best of them, and

> steal it from the rest of them; you know
> the score;
> Their ethics are a bore.

He adds the refrain:

> Get down to business, Mr. Businessman; if
> you can
> Before it's too late and you throw your life
> away.

No matter who we are or what our trade, we need to heed this song's warning lest we find this to be our epitaph:

> When you come down to it
> He really didn't know
> How to speak of profit
> Or what to count as loss.[1]

There is no way we can slough off this problem as irrelevant when we know we live in a society where wheeling and dealing is a way of life and where personal responsibility towards those who get stepped on is persistently denied. What makes us think we are immune from the values all around us? We are all under the pressure of wanting a little bigger slice of the pie. We all have our problems in confronting a materialistic value system.

---

[1] Words and music by Ray Stevens. © 1968 Ahab Music Co., Inc.

The Wheeler-Dealer

To address this problem we shift our attention to a man who played a key role in the life of Jacob. His name was Laban, Jacob's father-in-law. All the Bible commentaries say the same thing about Laban. He was one of the most crafty, slippery, and greedy men ever to walk across the pages of sacred history. He could have fit easily into the jungle of today's business world. He was a wheeler-dealer par excellence. One way or another, your value to him was always measured in what he could get out of you.

For Laban it had already started way back at the time when Abraham sent his servants and a camel train to his house to find a wife for Isaac. When Laban's sister, Rebekah, came running home to Laban, showing the gifts the servants had given when they met her at the well, Laban broke all existing records in getting out to meet those servants. He gave Rebekah's hand to Isaac in marriage, but not before his own hands were filled with gold and precious gifts.

Laban had not changed in the slightest when Jacob, Rebekah's son, arrived on the scene. Remembering the gift-laden camels of another day, Laban rushed out to greet Jacob. Business was looking up! But Jacob was alone. No retinue of gift-bearing servants accompanied him. It is true that Laban greeted Jacob with a kiss and an embrace; but Rashi, one of the most revered of all ancient Jewish commentators, wryly remarks that Laban, seeing that Jacob was alone, embraced him to see if he might not be carrying gold beneath his tunic and kissed him to see if he might not have pearls in his mouth!

Do we smile at this picture? If we do, it is probably out of recognition of our own tendency to ask, "What's going to be in this for me? If you say there is nothing, then forget it!" We all know how to figure what is profit and what is loss.

Don't Blame Me, Blame the System

Laban was also the prototype for all those who exploit people who cannot protect themselves and then pass it off as "what everybody does." When Jacob, through Laban's neat trick of now-you-see-her-now-you-don't flimflammery, woke up to find out that he had Leah in his tent instead of his beloved Rachel, he rushed out and protested this deceit to Laban. Laban then gave a classic demonstration of how to deny personal responsibility. With what was no doubt an extremely sad countenance Laban explained to Jacob that he really had no choice. He was bound by the customs of his society. When he promised to set things right, he reinforced his claim of not being personally responsible by saying, "We" (that is, he and the members of his community) "will give you the other one also in return for serving me another seven years" (Gen. 29:27).

How often, when caught in the middle of some fast dealing, a person is heard to say sheepishly, "Well, that's just the way things are done. You can be sure that if it had depended only on me, it would have been much different! But I am only one small individual. I can't fight the whole system."

The Jews of modern Israel, vividly aware of the Holocaust of World War II, have reflected more than most people on the excuses by which so many have disclaimed responsibility for the crimes against humanity which have swept over the modern world. One of their commentaries sums up the problem this way:

Man splits himself in two, into his personal "I" who does good and is acceptable and pleasant in the eyes of his friends, and the "I" which is but a cog in the anonymous public machine, be it the state of which he is but a functionary and servant, the army of which he is but one of the rank and file, the enterprise which he does not direct but merely serves. What blame can therefore be attached to him? He personally did not commit this iniquitous offense, but, on the contrary, always does favours to people. As a tiny membrane, however, in that gigantic anonymous body he is forced to do what is imposed on him and is not responsible *(Genesis,* Studies in Bereshit, p. 318).

Laban was a real expert in dodging responsibility for what he had done. The chances are that he knew something of what had caused Jacob to land on his doorstep alone and penniless. If he did, then he was actually needling Jacob when he told him that in *his* country it was not the custom for the younger to get a blessing before the older. It is not unlikely that Laban said to himself, "Well, this young rascal deserves whatever he gets. After all, if he had lived right, he wouldn't be in such a predicament." It is always so easy to make out that the victim is really the guilty one and only getting what he deserves. Like Laban we all love to shift the blame in order to protect our profit and avoid any loss.

"I'm Not in This for My Health, You Know"

"I'm not in this for my health, you know. I've got to think of my profit before I can think of your loss." Are these the excuses that blot out every other consideration? They were certainly the foundation for Laban's way of life. Under these ground rules he used the purchase price for his daughters for his own comforts. Before it was over they both complained that he had treated them like foreigners, not daughters (Gen. 31:15). He also used Jacob's labors for 20 years without giving him a share in the fruits of those labors. Why should he? Jacob could not retaliate. He was alone. He had no family or powerful friends to demand that justice be done. He was in the position typical of the poor. It was only much later, when Laban tried to do in Jacob one last time, that the Lord intervened and enabled Jacob to get some advantage.

It was at the time of their final heated exchange that Jacob let loose with his most stinging indictment of Laban. Conceivably, Jacob could have let loose with the charge that Laban was an idolator, for Laban was frantically accusing him of having stolen his household gods. Instead, Jacob cooly dismissed them as mere "household goods" (Gen. 31:37). True to the traditional Old Testament measurement of holiness, Jacob concentrated on what Laban had done to take advantage of a poor and helpless stranger. This is always where Hebrew ethics begins. Consider the judgment on Sodom and

Gomorrah. We usually regard the great shame of those cities as being connected with their sexual perversity. However, when Ezekiel the prophet pinpointed the cause for God's great anger against those cities, he cited something else. He said that the outcry against them (cf. Gen. 18:20-21) which merited their destruction was not their status as the "porno" capitals of the world. Sodom's greatest shame was that it had "pride, surfeit of God, and prosperous ease, but did not aid the poor and needy" (Ezek. 16:49). Their exploitation of the poor and their greater concern for their own profit than for the loss suffered by others placed them under the wrath of God even more than their practice of sodomy.

An Empty Man

Before Jacob left Laban for the last time, they erected a pile of stones and pledged to one another what to this day is called the *Mizpah:* "The Lord watch between you and me, when we are absent one from the other" (Gen. 31:49). In some gatherings it has come to be a form of sentimental leave-taking, but when Laban and Jacob said it they were indicating their wish that the Lord stand watch between them so that neither would any longer try to do the other in (Gen. 31:46-54). So Jacob was very definitely writing Laban out of his life. He was leaving Laban to face a fate which has befallen so many today: to become rich but lonely, calculating but devoid of vision, and hopelessly confused as to what in life is profit and what is loss.

Changing the Bottom Line

But now we ought to look at the other man central to our meditations on the life of Jacob. What we have said about Laban was not said to enjoy the gleeful condemnation of someone much worse than ourselves. It was said to show the kind of charges which can be laid against our own record of exploitation and selfishness. We have looked at Laban in order to see more clearly the need for Jesus' visit to this planet to set us all on a new path and to give us all a new understanding of what really needs to be written on the bottom line of our life's account.

We look to Jesus and ask, Did he ever meet people like Laban; and if he did, did he bother with them? The answer comes by remembering those money-hungry tax-collectors Jesus frequently dined with in the gospel accounts. For instance, he ate with Zacchaeus. Jesus was passing through Jericho, that lovely jewel in the desert and winter resort of kings, when he spied the chief tax collector, and cried out,

"Zacchaeus! Come down! I'm going to stay at your house today!" Make no mistake—Zacchaeus was not, as some Sunday school songs seem to suggest, an insignificant man. He may have been short, but he was "Mr. IRS" for one of the choicest territories in all Palestine; and everyone knew where he got the money for his fine house. Yet Jesus, only a few days away from his death on the cross, and knowing full well what awaited him as he went up from Jericho to Jerusalem for the last time, still had time for this money-grabber. He was showing that his Father had time, too. He was saying to you and me through this act, "And I would stay at *your* house today." As we have seen repeatedly, this is what the message of the Bible is all about. God takes the initiative in seeking out sinners who have cut themselves off from him.

What happens when God in his mercy lets us know that he will stay with us? We know what happened to Zacchaeus. His ideas about what was profit and what was loss began to change radically. He found the power for a changed life as he heard Jesus tell him that, despite his past record, he too was a son of Abraham and therefore had a share in the promises of God. That same power can be ours. Zacchaeus began to think about the poor, a group he had quite successfully ignored up to that point. He announced that he was going to give half of what he owned. No court of law had put Zacchaeus under indictment, but he nevertheless began to think about making restitution to those he had exploited. When God has visited us, no one needs to tell us to do these things. Our understanding of profit and loss has changed. We have been visited by the mercy of God. What more do we need? When God in Christ has filled the emptiness of our lives, we want to fill the lives of others.

In this season of Lent, as we review Jesus' journey up to Jerusalem to become the sacrifice for the sins of all, we can hear God saying directly to us, "I want to come and stay at your house today!" This is the declaration which can change your whole outlook concerning what is profit and what is loss. Friend, crawl down from your high perch on the ladder of success and welcome him. Jesus wants to stay with you today!

³ And Jacob sent messengers before him to Esau his brother in the land of Seir, the country of Edom, ⁴ instructing them, "Thus you shall say to my lord Esau: Thus says your servant Jacob, 'I have sojourned with Laban, and stayed until now; ⁵ and I have oxen, asses, flocks, menservants, and maidservants; and I have sent to tell my lord, in order that I may find favor in your sight.'"

⁶ And the messengers returned to Jacob, saying, "We came to your brother Esau, and he is coming to meet you, and four hundred men with him." ⁷ Then Jacob was greatly afraid and distressed; and he divided the people that were with him, and the flocks and herds and camels, into two companies, ⁸ thinking, "If Esau comes to the one company and destroys it, then the company which is left will escape."

⁹ And Jacob said, "O God of my father Abraham and God of my father Isaac, O Lord who didst say to me, 'Return to your country and to your kindred, and I will do you good,' ¹⁰ I am not worthy of the least of all the steadfast love and all the faithfulness which thou hast shown to thy servant, for with only my staff I crossed this Jordan; and now I have become two companies. ¹¹ Deliver me, I pray thee, from the hand of my brother, from the hand of Esau, for I fear him, lest he come and slay us all, the mothers with the children. ¹² But thou didst say, 'I will do you good, and make your descendants as the sand of the sea, which cannot be numbered for multitude.'"

Genesis 32:3-12
Parallel readings: Ps. 102:1-17; Rom. 8:26-39

5

The Step Up to Courage

**Finding a way for courage
to become the companion of my fears**

In this Lenten season of self-examination we turn again to the problem of being people who do the will of God. We have already examined our dangerous tendency to confuse our will with God's will, but that is not the only form this problem takes. Often we know very well what God wants us to do, but we find it a hard way to follow. God has a way of asking us to take a risk or pay a price we would just as soon avoid. He confronts us with difficult decisions which demand a level of courage we are not sure we have.

Courage Never Comes Easily

It takes courage to place our future or the future of our loved ones totally into the hands of God. It takes courage to agree to surgery. It takes courage to withstand the pressure of public opinion and take a stand when the one whose will we feel called to obey seems totally absent from the field of battle. It takes courage to accept the evidence that now may be the time to die.

Courage in the face of such demands does not come because we know in advance that nothing serious is really going to happen anyway. If we have that kind of advance knowledge, we do not need courage. Courage comes into its own only when we do not know what will happen and are frightened by this knowledge. Carroll E. Simcox quotes that crusty hero, Eddie Rickenbacker, on this basic fact of life: "Courage is doing what you're afraid to do. There can be no courage unless you're scared" *(A Treasury of Quotations on Christian Themes,* p. 163). We are told about Moses that "by faith he left Egypt, not being afraid of the anger of the king; for he endured as seeing him who is invisible" (Heb. 11:27). But how shall we find such courage? We need to wrestle with God over this question because, as C.S. Lewis has remarked, courage is not simply one of many virtues. It is the quality which marks every other virtue at its moment of testing.

Courage did not come easily to Jacob, the

man through whom we have been gaining a better understanding of our own struggles with God. At this point in his life, he was once again terribly afraid. He had entered into the land of Edom and knew that soon he would meet his brother. He had known this fear once before, when he had bedded down at Bethel as he fled the wrath of Esau. Now as he reentered his homeland 20 years later, nothing seemed to have changed. He was still afraid of Esau. Jacob had sent gift-bearing messengers ahead to demonstrate his friendship and goodwill, but they had returned with bad news. Esau was marching toward Jacob, accompanied by 400 armed men. More than Jacob's wealth was at stake. Esau and his army might kill the entire family.

Prayer as a Resource for Courage

The conflict between Jacob and Esau seemed unchanged, but Jacob had begun to change from the man he had once been. He was able to offer up to God the kind of prayer through which courage is born. It was not an ornate prayer. He began by speaking simply and directly to the "God of my father Abraham and God of my father Isaac" (Gen. 32:9). At one time Jacob's will had been all that mattered. Now the will of God mattered more. He was obeying

God, who told him, "Return to your country and to your kindred, and I will do you good." At one time Jacob thought he deserved the world with a ribbon around it. Now he thought and prayed about what little claim he had on God's favor, saying, "I am not worthy of the least of all the steadfast love and all the faithfulness which thou hast shown to thy servant, for with only my staff I crossed this Jordan; and now I have become two companies." He knew that all this was now up for grabs, and honestly confessed his feelings, saying of Esau, "I fear him, lest he come and slay us all, the mothers with the children" (Gen. 32:10-11).

The situation was desperate. Jacob did not know just how things would turn out, but he was pressing towards that inner strength which comes from beyond ourselves. His fears were real, but the entrance of courage became possible because now Jacob began to claim the promises of God. He said to the Lord, "But thou didst say, 'I will do you good, and make your descendants as the sand of the sea, which cannot be numbered for multitude'" (Gen. 32:12).

Jacob had to struggle with God in prayer in order to tap the courage he needed. So did Jesus. Of all the pictures of a man wrestling with God in prayer, none is more vivid than that of our Lord in the Garden of Gethsemane. He, too, spoke directly and yet passionately. Jesus said, "Abba, Father!", which means, "O Father, dear Father!" (Mark 14:36). That phrase reflected a confidence in God which would sustain him until he said from the cross, "Father, into thy hands I commit my spirit!" (Luke 23:46). For him, too, the terrors ahead were awesome. He "prayed that, if it were possible, the hour might pass from him" (Mark 14:35). But his Father's will was most important of all. "Yet not what I will, but what thou wilt" (Mark 14:36).

Recalling this scene at Gethsemane, the writer to the Hebrews explains what was happening: "In the days of his flesh, Jesus offered up prayers and supplications, with loud cries and tears, to him who was able to save him from death, and he was heard for his godly fear. Although he was a Son, he learned obedience through what he suffered; and being made perfect, he became the source of eternal salvation to all who obey him . . ." (Heb. 5:7-9). The removal of the cup before him was not to be God's answer to Jesus' fear. The Father's answer lay in giving him the strength and courage to see it through; and because Jesus received that courage, he became a perfect sacrifice and the source of salvation for all who will commit themselves to him. That salvation includes giving you and me the courage to hold on to the promises of God in the face of the terrors before us. Think of Jesus—the pioneer and perfecter of our faith—the writer to the Hebrews urges, "and then you will not give up for want of courage" (Heb. 12:2-3 JB).

The Gift of Prayer

If Lent is a time for self-examination, it is also a time for that renewal of strength which comes through prayer. But the paradox we face is that while help will come to those who struggle in prayer, such prayer is always the gift of the Holy Spirit. This is God's word of promise and hope: "Likewise the Spirit helps us in our weakness; for we do not know how to pray as we ought, but the Spirit himself intercedes for us with sighs too deep for words" (Rom. 8:26). We have the promise that the Spirit will help us come into contact with the source of all life and power. The Spirit will give us the same kind of courage Jesus found in the moment of his testing. We are not whistling in the dark when we say this. Jesus himself has promised this help. He told his disciples, "Do not be anxious how or what you are to answer or what you are to say; for the Holy Spirit will teach

you in that very hour what you ought to say"
(Luke 12:11-12).

A young pastor discovered how the Spirit
can become the guide to courage-producing
prayer just when he needed it most. Although
it was not consciously planned that way, it resulted in an experience and prayer whose content was remarkably like the experience of
Jacob. It is an example of a man learning the
hard way, as Jacob did.

This young pastor's ministry was being sabo-
taged by a man whose destructive effect on the
Lord's work was nothing short of demonic.
Eventually, in fact, that man was placed on
the FBI's "Ten Most Wanted" list. The pastor
did not know what to do. He felt completely alone. If the car driven by this antagonist
crossed his path, he would feel his stomach
tighten up in knots. Preaching became an or-
deal, sound sleep a forgotten experience, and
eating difficult because of a constricted throat.
He had many of the symptoms of profound
anxiety.

Finally, after being unable to eat his Saturday
evening meal or concentrate on the next day's
services, he drove out of the city to a side road.
There, in a struggle in which it seemed that
every word had to be hammered out individ-
ually, he began to write out a prayer. It was not

a long prayer, but that is not unusual. Many of the prayers of the Bible, like the prayers of Jacob and Jesus, are very short; but this does not mean that these people prayed only for a minute or two. Sometimes you can pray all night with deep sighs and groanings and yet the words, if put down on paper, may be few in number.

In that prayer he put his future into God's hands. He confessed both his fears and his faults. He put things into perspective. He gave thanks for God's many blessings, especially giving thanks for his wife. He promised God that he would stop wallowing in self-pity and rededicate himself to his calling. He wrote that he believed the Lord had much work still in mind for him and concluded, "Help me to keep the perspective of my whole life in your service and not just think that these days are my whole life. If you lead me you will show me the way to go. I ask you to lead me." Like Jacob of old, he was beginning to lay claim to the promises of God. But he never claimed it was a prayer of his own making. It was a prayer brought forth by the Holy Spirit.

When the prayer was finished, this young man felt a surge of power. He turned on the ignition and sped home. Late at night he ate a huge dinner and then slept like a baby. He preached with joy and conviction the next morning. Courage had returned because he had learned to trust in someone greater than himself. With this new outlook he also found human support surrounding him that he had previously failed to recognize. I know this, for I was that pastor.

I do not claim this to be an exceptional testimony. I tell it as a reminder of how the same kind of experience has taken place in the life of just about every one of us, and how that experience can come again through the help of God's Spirit. Sometimes we let our heart become like a closed and stuffy room—the atmosphere choked with the smell of fear. Then, although we do not know how to pray as we ought, we begin; and what the Old Testament calls the *ruach* of God —his breath, his spirit—sweeps into our heart, and the air becomes fresh again.

It is true, we are easily made fearful and our prayers uncertain. But it does not have to remain that way. As the story of Jacob shows us, rascals can change, sinners can become sanctified, and the irreligious can learn how to pray. Above all, we know we can grow because God has made his promise that in the moment of testing the Spirit will help us to pray. Prayer is his gift, and in our hesitant and timid reaching out we discover this truth once more. The presence of him who wrestled in prayer at Gethsemane fills our heart, and we have the power to quiet our fears.

He not only shows us the Father's will—he gives us the courage to follow it.

The story of Jacob gave birth to the spiritual, "We Are Climbing Jacob's Ladder." Where are you today on this ladder of life? Wherever you are, through prayer you can take the step up to courage.

²² The same night he arose and took his two wives, his two maids, and his eleven children, and crossed the ford of the Jabbok. ²³ He took them and sent them across the stream, and likewise everything that he had. ²⁴ And Jacob was left alone; and a man wrestled with him until the breaking of the day.

Genesis 32:22-24
Parallel readings: Ps. 77:4-15; Matt. 26:69—27:10

6

Must I Be Alone?

**The problem of estrangement
in our modern society**

A front-page news feature began with these words:

At 10 o'clock in the morning, Frances Compton opens her apartment window and drops a shopping bag, with a string tied to it, onto Academy Street below.

Frances Compton is getting her mail.

The 74-year-old woman has been using the shopping bag and string to get both her mail and her afternoon paper for years. She doesn't like going out on Academy Street. She is afraid to go out on Academy Street.

The frail, slightly stooped woman, who still wears her white hair in curls, has been afraid since her purse was stolen from her, right on her front steps.

Mrs. Compton feels isolated. . . .

Old age and fear have barricaded Mrs. Compton in two cluttered rooms on Academy Street.

Trenton Times, Jan. 5, 1977

Isolated Because of Broken Relationships

This little lady is a dramatic but not unusual example of the growing number of people who find themselves isolated from others. We used to think of this as a malady confined to depressed urban areas. Now it has also spread to suburban areas. It is even reaching out into small towns and rural areas where people have lost their old confidence in their neighbors.

A sense of isolation is overtaking people everywhere, both within the family and outside the home. People trying to make it as parents, children, marriage partners, workers, employers, teachers, students, or members of the Christian church feel cut off and alone. There are walls everywhere. If we are honest, we know that we have built many of them ourselves. We have frozen people out of our circle of responsibility and then have gone to great lengths to prove that they deserved being ostracized. We have argued that they disqualified themselves by their own choice. Others have done the same to us.

This is why books about parents and children overcoming loneliness, learning to communicate, fighting fair, and managing conflict become best-sellers. We are all dealers in pain, and we all ache for a way out of the alienation and isolation which we have both created and suffered from.

As we seek to understand this human condition we find ourselves looking again at the experiences of Jacob. In simple eloquence Scripture tells us, "And Jacob was left alone. . . ." I can feel his sense of isolation in my bones. I can understand it. Who can possibly look back at what happened between him and Isaac, or Esau, or his wives, or Laban, or his sons, and not see why he was so alone? The long road of his life had been strewn with the wreckage of broken relationships. Sitting in the inky darkness beside the River Jabbok, he was alone in the deepest sense of the word, feeling isolated from both his fellows and from God.

A terrible thing happens to us when fellowship is destroyed. We catch a glimpse of its consequences also in the closing hours of Jesus' life. We see Judas standing outside the city, a rope in his hands. When he slipped away from the loving relationship which had been offered to him in the Upper Room, the account grimly concludes, "and it was night" (John 13:30). It was a night that never ended for him. When he tried to undo what he had done, his new partners shrugged off his confession. "What is that to us? See to it yourself" (Matt. 27:4). As far as they were concerned his feeling of guilt was his problem, not theirs. So Judas hanged himself. He felt that only death was willing to embrace him.

We see Peter crawling away to weep alone over the way he had denied his fellowship with the Master (Matt. 26:75). We think of the disciples in isolation from one another as they stare into the dead ashes of the fire which had burned out during the night of Jesus' arrest and trial, a night in which they had forsaken him and fled. The fire had gone out in them, as well. It always does when we destroy the fellowship God has given us. This we have all done. We all stand condemned. We stand alone.

Our Isolation Shattered

But as we have seen time and again, God simply will not leave us alone. We may not be able to break out of our isolation, but God breaks into it. Jacob found this out one more time. "And a man wrestled with him until the breaking of the day" (Gen. 32:24). There had been no noise at all except for the faint ripple of the stream, when out of the darkness a being emerged and seized Jacob. Jacob grappled with him. There is really nothing quite like it in the entire Bible. What was happening? The prophet Hosea explains it by saying, "In his manhood he (Jacob) strove with God" (Hos. 12:3-4). But granting the possibility of a wrestling match with a spirit-being, what does it *mean*?

The book of The Wisdom of Solomon (in the Apocrypha) describes this event as Jacob's inner struggle with the "Wisdom" of God (10:9-12). Perhaps we feel we can understand a little better a reference to an inner struggle, but of first importance is understanding *why* this struggle came about. It was initiated by God. God sought out Jacob. God confronted him. He struggled with him. God taking the initiative is once more the theme of a chapter in Jacob's life, and we see again that the Bible does not tell about our search for God, but about God's search for us. It tells us how God finds men and women and makes them his own once again.

The same good news is at the core of the message about Jesus Christ. Indeed, the entire Old Testament is but a prelude to Jesus as the final revelation of the heart of God toward human beings. Here we are, people who have shut out brothers and sisters and even God himself, and then Christ slips into the dark night of our spiritual isolation and begins to grapple with us. He confronts us as one who was totally abandoned himself. We are reminded of his cry, "My God, my God, why have you deserted me?" (Matt. 27:46 JB). But he also tells us that because of his abandonment on the cross, our sins, which have hurt and cut off so many and ultimately have been a betrayal of the Lord of Love himself, shall not be charged against us. In Christ we discover that the everlasting arms of God which seize us do so in an embrace of love. We can't believe it. It's against all reason. He who struggles *with* us is he who struggles *for* us. It can be explained only in the manner chosen by the apostle Paul: this "weakness of God" is greater than the strength of the men who wrestle against him (1 Cor. 1:25). We must simply cry out, "Fight with me, O God! Don't ever let me go from the embrace of Christ. Fight on, for through you alone can a new life begin!"

No Longer Alone

No one need argue much about the reality of our isolation. The evidence is everywhere. But can we believe that through Christ we need never be alone again? Art critics say that in "The Last Supper" Leonardo da Vinci sought to portray Christ as one who was already forsaken and alone, thus exposing the artist's own feelings at this time in his career. No friend rests upon the bosom of Jesus. Every line in the painting stresses his isolation, an isolation he felt so deeply as he said, "The time is coming, and is already here, when all of you will be scattered, each one to his own home, and I will be left all alone." But then he continued with words so significant that we should never forget them: "But I am not really alone, because the Father is with me" (John 16:32 TEV). Now we can say that, too. We have met God in Christ, and he will never leave us.

But what about the little lady on Academy Street? Do we simply tell her not to feel too badly and to remember that she is not really alone because Jesus is with her? Never! If we think that this is the only conclusion we ought to be reaching, then we might as well be sitting at home listening to an evangelist while we lock all the doors and disconnect the doorbell so that no one can disturb us in our moment of lovely religious contemplation! To take this approach is to fall under the condemnation from the letter of James: "If a brother or sister is ill-clad and in lack of daily food, and one of you says to them, 'Go in peace, be warmed and filled,' without giving them the things needed for the body, what does it profit? So faith by itself, if it has no works, is dead" (James 2:15-17).

In the Bible life under the blessings of God is

always a life which overcomes the barriers which separate people from one another. Even in Jacob's case, it was the purpose of God that there be this struggle so that he would be ready to make genuine peace with his brother Esau and become a worthy father to those who would be the progenitors of the 12 tribes of Israel. To be specific, God embraces us so that we in turn will be able to embrace the little lady on Academy Street.

Sister Teresa, the saintly angel of God to the poorest of the poor in Calcutta, sums up the challenge when she says, "The biggest disease today is not leprosy or tuberculosis, but rather the feeling of being unwanted, uncared for, and deserted by everybody. The greatest evil is the lack of charity, the terrible indifference toward one's neighbor who lives at the roadside assaulted by exploitation, corruption, poverty and disease" (*Something Beautiful for God*, p. 55).

Her own response to this great sickness has been to take Christ at his word as he says, "I was hungry and you gave me food, I was thirsty and you gave me drink, I was a stranger and you welcomed me, I was naked and you clothed me, I was sick and you visited me, I was in prison and you came to me" (Matt. 25:35-36). She has built her whole life on the principle that in serving the forgotten, especially those forgotten and abandoned by *everyone,* we are serving him; and this conviction has resulted in a miracle of love unsurpassed in all the world.

In serving the forgotten, we are serving Christ. Some sophisticates, always ready to find fault with the morality of the Bible, say that we would be on a higher moral plane if we did something for a fellow human being simply because of human need, not because it is done for Christ. But there is no Sister Teresa among them. It is easy to question the motivations of others, but it is far better to believe with all simplicity what Jesus has said, and find him where he says he can be found. Today you can moisten his parched lips. Today you can ease his hunger and clothe his broken body. Today you can welcome him, a stranger, into your circle of love. You can visit him today where he lies upon a hospital cot or sits behind bars. Yes, this day you can find Jesus in what Sister Teresa calls his "distressing disguise."

It is a terrible thing to be left alone. That is why jailers make solitary confinement their ultimate threat. But now Christ has come to set the prisoners free. He brings this about as he comes to us in not one but three ways. As God came to Jacob, so through Christ he breaks in on my isolation and will not let me go. Through his Spirit he dwells in my heart, impelling me to become a "little Christ" to others; and in the sublimest mystery of all, he lives among the forgotten of this world, that I might serve him still. So through Christ our isolation is ended forevermore.

^{24} And Jacob was left alone; and a man wrestled with him until the breaking of the day. ^{25} When the man saw that he did not prevail against Jacob, he touched the hollow of his thigh; and Jacob's thigh was put out of joint as he wrestled with him. ^{26} Then he said, "Let me go, for the day is breaking." But Jacob said, "I will not let you go, unless you bless me." ^{27} And he said to him, "What is your name?" And he said, "Jacob." ^{28} Then he said, "Your name shall no more be called Jacob, but Israel, for you have striven with God and with men, and have prevailed." ^{29} Then Jacob asked him, "Tell me, I pray, your name." But he said, "Why is it that you ask my name?" And there he blessed him.

Genesis 32:24-29
Parallel readings: Ps. 22:1-24; John 19:17-30

7

At Last I Know My Name (Good Friday)

The discovery of my real identity through Christ

There is only one place to go on Good Friday: the foot of the cross. Perhaps on this more than on any one other day of the year, people do make that pilgrimage. But for how long and with what feelings? Even now more people are crowding the malls shopping for Easter finery. It seems that so often when there is a great religious festival celebrating what God has given to us, people have a corresponding urge to go on a splurge of buying for themselves. Could it be that they are afraid they have missed the gift and can be reassured of their identity only through the possession of things?

In any event, the crowds on the mall in a larger sense reflect the spiritual condition of our times. Life itself is like a giant mall filled with people shopping around for something new, and on both sides there are shop signs urging people to enter their doors. "Do you want to find yourself?" they ask. "Then come in to us." The people enter, and then we hear them saying they are "into" Zen, or EST, or astrology, or biofeedback, or revival in our time. In one door and out the other, in the next door and out again, we hear them explaining, "I'm still trying to find myself."

The hunger to find oneself is not to be despised. We all have this need. In fact throughout the Lenten season we have been looking at one particular man who was trying to find himself. His name was Jacob. If you have not been with us up to this point, it might seem strange to be talking about a patriarch of the Old Testament on Good Friday; but in his experiences we have a beautiful model of how we, too, can find ourselves—not along a riverbank, but beneath the cross of Jesus.

On a night when the darkness was much like the darkness of Good Friday, Jacob heard a question we all must answer. God had engaged him in a night-long encounter. When Jacob asked for a blessing, he heard God ask, "What is your name?" He replied, "Jacob." The name *Jacob* means, first of all, "a wrestler," or refers to a wrestling hold. Jacob could claim that name with authority. He had figuratively pinned many ad-

versaries during his lifetime. He had bested everyone he met from Esau to Laban. But on this
night he was confronted by the holy presence of
God. When this form of divine being grappled
with him and asked him his name, I believe that
a second meaning of that name emerged and
filled Jacob's mind. The name also means, "the
supplanter." I believe that at that point, as he
said his name, his whole life passed before him.
He saw his tricks against Esau, Isaac, and Laban.
He recalled his lack of love toward members of
his family and became aware of his self-centered
life. Yes, he could point to a life of many accom-
plishments, a life graced by the blessings of God.
But now as he said his name, he realized how
much it stood for the wrong in his life. Shame
filled him as he said, "My name is Jacob." In
giving his name he was confessing the kind of
person he had been.

What Is Your Name?

In this service of growing darkness, I want
you to hear as never before this same question:
"What is your name?" Your name is important
to you, and no doubt certain outstanding accom-
plishments can be attached to it, but we ought
to look at it more closely tonight. God is confronting you at this moment, and it is he who

asks your name. What is it? I want you to say your name to yourself and let the saying of it be an act of self-awareness. Let your name speak to you of your missing the mark, or omitting what ought to have been done, or having crossed over the borderline between right and wrong. It is eternally important that you know who you are as you stand before God. If you, like Jacob, are in a struggle to find yourself and the blessing of God, you must tell him your name. It is an axiom of the faith that before there can be a blessing there must be confession. Before we can be lifted up we must be humbled.

We must say our name. We must say it before the cross, where people disputed whether or not there should be added to the name of Jesus the title "King of the Jews." But while the argument goes on about the significance of his name, he looks down from the cross, and with the voice of God asks all of us beneath it, "What is your name?" We must say, "I am Jacob."

Finding a New Name

Confessing who we are is only the first step in finding ourselves, for that expression suggests a discovery of something we did not know before. We look again at Jacob. How fully human he was! Jewish people might say that he was "a real *mensch*." He was a scoundrel and a saint. He often tried to slip away from God; and yet when confronted at last, he had the courage to ask for that which he knew was his greatest need: the blessing of the fulness of God's presence resting upon him. He told God he wouldn't let go until he got this blessing. But had not God invaded Jacob's life and seized him in the darkness because it was his intention to bless him all along? So the Lord said, "We have struggled together and you have confessed who you are. Now I shall give you the blessing you desire. You are someone new, and as that new person you belong to me. I am giving you a new name. You shall no longer be called 'Jacob' but 'Israel.' "

Israel means, "He who strives with God." But Jacob did not earn that name, and certainly not because he had fought so well. There would have been no encounter at all if God had not intervened once more in his life. As the life of Jacob shows repeatedly, the Old and New Testaments have but one gospel. It is the story of God mercifully intervening in the lives of sinners. Now Jacob knew that he had not only a regrettable past, but also a new and exciting future. For years he had sought to find himself. Over the span of a full generation he had tried to find out how he fit in the plans of God. I can see him bursting with joy as he whispered to himself, "At last I know my name!"

With Jacob's joyful discovery fresh in our minds, we think again about our own reasons for gathering together on Good Friday. The message of this day should always be simple and unadorned. It is a time for holding up the work God was carrying out through the cross of his Son. It is a time for applying the meaning of that cross to our lives. When Pilate refused to change the inscription above the cross which announced that Jesus was King of the Jews, saying, "What I have written I have written" (John 19:22), this did not prove that he knew the meaning of what was happening. But *you* can know. Jacob wanted to know the name of the one with whom he struggled. Now in Jesus we have learned his name—and more. This same Jesus who became the true Israel and died on our behalf has done more than reveal the name of God. In Jesus God has revealed his heart. It is a heart of love for sinners. That heart of love is so great that the only-begotten Son—he who *was* God and was *with* God—laid down his life to take away the guilt of our sins. Because Jesus is this expression of the perfect love of God, he has now been given a "name which is above every name, that at the name of Jesus every knee should bow . . . and every tongue confess that Jesus Christ is Lord . . . (Phil. 2:9-11).

This same Jesus now speaks to you from the cross. He speaks with the voice of God, but this time he does not ask your name. He gives new meaning to it. He gives a new identity to you who have been trying to find yourself. He is the Good Shepherd who "calls his own sheep by name and leads them out" (John 10:3). He is the Father's personal guarantee of that wonderful promise first spoken through Isaiah: "Fear not, for I have redeemed you; I have called you by name, you are mine" (Isa. 43:1). You who have faith in him can know that your name is written in the book of life, and that this name shall not be removed (Phil. 4:3; Luke 10:20).

I suppose there are people who might want to say the Bible is the story of people who found themselves. I can understand what they are trying to say, but it is really better to say that it is the story of people found by God and made new again: Jacob on the banks of the River Jabbok, Saul on the road to Damascus, Isaiah meditating in the temple, and Galilean fishermen occupied with cleaning their nets. The newness of life which really matters is not something people make happen, but rather something that happens *to* them.

It can happen to you sitting in church tonight.

God is calling to you. He asks your name. He wants to know what you have been doing. Then he invites you to the foot of the cross to receive there the blessing of Christ as your Savior and Lord. This is how you can discover the real you, the new you. This is how you can help others find themselves, too, so that we can observe Easter's joy with this song of thanksgiving already on our lips: "Thanks to Jesus, I know my name. I know who I am!"

²⁸ Then he said, "Your name shall no more be called Jacob, but Israel, for you have striven with God and with men, and have prevailed." ²⁹ Then Jacob asked him, "Tell me, I pray, your name." But he said, "Why is it that you ask my name?" And there he blessed him. ³⁰ So Jacob called the name of the place Peniel, saying, "For I have seen God face to face, and yet my life is preserved." ³¹ The sun rose upon him as he passed Penuel, limping because of his thigh.

Genesis 32:28-31
Parallel readings: Ps. 118:1-25; Matt. 28:1-10

8

That Yet More Glorious Day (Easter)

**The need for hope
in a hopeless society**

In the years when isolated sanatoriums were still the only answer for people suffering from tuberculosis, I had a conversation with a woman afflicted with the dread disease. Drawing upon a phrase from the book of Psalms which I will never forget, she nodded toward the window and said in a voice edged with despair, "Out there, that's the 'land of the living.' " She still walked and breathed, but already she was dead to hope.

Dead to Hope and Dead to God

The struggle to believe that through the help of God there lies ahead what the hymn "For All the Saints" calls "a yet more glorious day" is still with us today. A case in point is the recent disclosure that among the young the second most common cause of death is not some lethal disease or the wanton use of drugs or alcohol. It is suicide. Only accidental deaths outrank it, and no one knows how many times an "accident" was not a conscious or subconscious effort by a young person to end it all. Psychiatrists say that while in some cases the stress of life may have been severe, the growing trend in suicides is not due to the increase of stress. They pinpoint the cause as a depression which, in their own words, has left young people feeling that there is "no one to trust." These young people have given up on life. They believe in no one. There is for them no possibility of "a yet more glorious day." They are already in the midst of death. Nor are they the exception on an otherwise tranquil national scene. They are rather a reflection of adult emptiness all around them. In our nation today the inventory of hope is pitifully low. The shelves marked "hope," "confidence," and "vision" are almost bare. Millions are dead to hope and dead to God.

During this past Lenten season we have been studying the life of a man who came just about as close to being dead to hope and to God as a person can come. He was the Hebrew patriarch Jacob, a man whose life was filled with the experiences familiar to all of us. You know something of what he felt and experienced if you have faced what seems to be the dead-end of your highest hopes, if you have been placed against your will in a strange and unwanted situation, if you have feared that years of hard work were about to go up in smoke before your very eyes, or if someone very dear to you has been threatened with death. Most significantly of all, Jacob at last had come to a point in his life where he had to face the truth that he had not been living for God but for himself. It was a point at which he could have used the words uttered by another great person of God, St. Augustine, as he looked back on his past: "Such was my life. Was that life?" The answer was, No! Much that we call life is not life. It is death. Life is not doing your own thing. Life is doing God's thing. When either my despair or my decisions deny God's lordship over my life, I have chosen death. I am dead. I am cut off from the land of the living.

New Life through Seeing God

Something happened to Jacob which brought him back to the land of the living. It made him a brand-new person. It was not because of something he did. It was something that happened *to* him. God thrust himself into Jacob's empty and fear-ridden life. In a merciful act of forgiveness and renewal God gave Jacob a new identity and a new name. He said that Jacob should henceforth be called "Israel."

In utter joy and amazement Jacob responded by saying, "I have seen God face to face . . ." (Gen. 32:30). Any explanation of this statement must go far deeper than a claim that if only Jacob had owned a Polaroid Land camera with flash attachment, he could have whipped out his prints and said to the people back at his camp, "Look right here, I've got a picture of God!" The statement "I have seen God face to face" means much more than that or it means nothing at all. A scholar in Middle Eastern anthropology explains that this phrase is linked to a common expression in that region. When someone says that they live "beneath the face" of another, it means that they live under them as their servant, trusting in their protection. When Jacob makes this kind of statement he is saying, "God has become real to me. I know him now. I know I can entrust everything to him, and I shall serve him with all my heart."

"We have seen God face to face in Jesus" is also the joyful claim of every believer on Easter morn. The good news of this day is that once and for all God has disclosed himself through Jesus Christ. Think of that first Easter. At dawn, frightened and sorrowing women had come to apply spices to a dead body. Instead they heard an angel say, "Do not be afraid; for I know that you seek Jesus who was crucified. He is not here; for he has risen, as he said" (Matt. 28:5-7). Jesus had returned to the land of the living and by that return brought with him new hope! Two disciples, heads bowed with grief, were met by Jesus on the road to Emmaus. They did not know him—not until he broke bread with them. Then their eyes were opened, and they rushed to tell the others. Step by step the New Testament shows us the followers of Jesus excitedly passing the word, first in whispers, then from the very housetops. Jesus had brought back to them the hope that for all of them there lay ahead "a yet more glorious day."

It had seemed at first that God had turned away from Jesus. It looked as if sinful men had gotten Jesus down and were going to keep him down; but even as the name *Israel* means "he who strives with God," Jesus was the true and perfect Israel. He strove *with* God and *for* God in order to redeem those who were lost. Like Jacob of old, he who appeared pinned by death came forth stronger than ever. Through that struggle he paid for the wages of sin for all people and broke the bonds of death. That is the meaning of his resurrection.

Today God speaks to us as he once spoke to Jacob. He says, "Yes, I love you, whoever you are and whatever your past. I have shown you this love in the face of my Son. I promise you that through him your name has become new and is written in the book of life." Seeing God is like going up from the valley of death into the land of the living, and the announcement of Christ's resurrection on Easter makes it possible for us to say, "I have seen God!" Jacob named the site of his encounter with God *Peniel*, which means, "the face of God." Today Jesus, because of his resurrection, has become *our* Peniel.

New Hope as We Face Life

Some years ago a powerful Broadway play, *Sunrise at Campobello,* told the story of polio striking down a young and vigorous Franklin Delano Roosevelt while he was at his remote summer home. His will to live was tested to the utmost. Then there was the question of whether to give up and retire to the life of a crippled gentleman farmer or return to public life. When at last these crises had been met and passed, he confessed that the fire he had gone through had tested the resources of his faith as nothing had before. Now he possessed new maturity and determination. He had become a cripple, yet he emerged a stronger man.

Our text tells us that Jacob took the same giant step of inner growth. He left his encounter with God afflicted with a lifelong limp which would always remind him of the intensity of his own personal struggle with God. But if he was a wounded and marked man, he was also a man able to meet the uncertainties still before him, beginning with the effort to be reconciled to a brother he had wronged terribly many years before. Jacob did not know what would happen. He only knew that it was his responsibility to seek reconciliation. He sought it armed only with trust that God would see him through. Jacob, who had been so contemptuous of Esau in his youth, stood at last before his brother. He bowed low to him. He made an offering of peace and told Esau that his forgiveness would be like seeing the face of God! (Gen. 33:10). They were reunited on the spot, and the sun had risen on a new day for Israel.

The sun has also risen on you this morning, and for each of us there is some step into life which we need to take with new boldness. It may be facing someone you have wronged, changing a habit, saying that you are sorry, giving up a false god, or even standing boldly before the angel of death. Each of us knows what such a step will mean personally, and we know that such ventures often demand what seems to be an awesome price. As we face such a choice, we would do well to remember that it is the victorious Jesus who has paved the way for us. He asks nothing of us that he did not demand of himself. As his enemies swooped down on him he said, "The world must be shown that I love the Father, and do exactly as he commands; so up, let us go forward!" (John 14:31 NEB). Through him we can actually love the step forward into the unknown where the Father wants us to go. Through him we can prefer it to the place we already know.

It is never easy to face the future, but we *can* face it when we have seen the face of God in the Easter dawn. A Christian woman went to the wake of an old and now departed friend. At the funeral home she met her friend's daughter. "Oh," she said, "It's so good to see you again, though I'm sorry it has to be under these circumstances." The daughter smiled and said, "On the contrary, while there is sadness, this is a wonderful moment! After all, mother has finally gained the victory!" This is what those who have seen the face of God can say.

One of the finest tributes to the significance of the life of Jacob lies in the simple yet profound spiritual, "We Are Climbing Jacob's Ladder." It sings of the upward struggle of God's people, and each verse ends addressing those pilgrims as "soldiers of the cross." Life is like that. The climb is not finished. The steps are not easy. The top of the ladder is still hidden in a cloud. But we press on. We do not see it yet, but we know the time is coming when we shall no longer see the glory of God dimly, as in a mirror, but face to face. For even now through the risen Christ we have seen his glory, and through him we are confident that there lies ahead of us "a yet more glorious day."